Interracial Marriage

Loving v. Virginia

CATHLEEN SMALL

Cavendish
Square

New York

Published in 2019 by Cavendish Square Publishing, LLC
243 5th Avenue, Suite 136, New York, NY 10016

Library of Congress Cataloging-in-Publication Data

Names: Small, Cathleen, author.
Title: Interracial marriage : Loving v. Virginia / Cathleen Small.
Description: New York : Cavendish Square, 2018. |
Series: Courting history | Includes bibliographical references and index.
Identifiers: LCCN 2018000186 (print) | LCCN 2018000891 (ebook) |
ISBN 9781502635877 (eBook) | ISBN 9781502635860 (library bound) |
ISBN 9781502635884 (pbk.)
Subjects: LCSH: Loving, Richard Perry--Trials, litigation, etc.--Juvenile literature. |
Loving, Mildred Jeter--Trials, litigation, etc.--Juvenile literature. |
Interracial marriage--Law and legislation--Virginia--Juvenile literature.
Classification: LCC KF224.L68 (ebook) | LCC KF224.
L68 S63 2018 (print) | DDC 346.7301/63--dc23
LC record available at https://lccn.loc.gov/2018000186

Editorial Director: David McNamara
Editor: Chet'la Sebree
Copy Editor: Nathan Heidelberger
Associate Art Director: Amy Greenan
Designer: Joseph Parenteau
Production Coordinator: Karol Szymczuk
Photo Research: J8 Media

Printed in the United States of America

Contents

ONE
Civil Rights, Interracial Marriage, and the Lovings

The United States Supreme Court's ruling on *Loving v. Virginia* came at the tail end of the civil rights movement. The civil rights movement was a social and political movement focused on securing equal rights for black people in the United States in the 1950s and 1960s. In the eighty years leading up to the civil rights movement, there were several court cases that established that interracial marriage, or the marriage between two people of different races, was illegal. These cases established legal precedents, or legal decisions used to help decide other cases. Despite the precedents, the US Supreme Court unanimously decided to vote in favor of interracial marriage in 1967. The ruling was a landmark decision. Landmark decisions are those that affect the way the court system interprets existing laws. The *Loving* decision was a sign of a shift against the tide of racism.

The Lovings

When the *Loving v. Virginia* case went before the Supreme Court, Richard Perry Loving and Mildred Delores Loving

Mildred (*left*) and Richard (*right*) Loving, circa 1965

were the plaintiffs. The Commonwealth of Virginia was the defendant. Originally, the Lovings were the defendants.

Mildred and Richard Loving were both from Virginia. Mildred was a black woman with Native American ancestry. Richard was a white man. When Mildred was eighteen and Richard was twenty-four, the couple married in Washington, DC. They went to DC to get married because interracial marriage was legal in the city. Interracial marriage was a crime in Virginia ever since the Racial Integrity Act of 1924. After marrying, they returned to their home in Virginia. When local police realized that the couple was married, they raided the Lovings' home in the middle of the night and arrested the husband and wife.

The Lovings avoided serving jail time by agreeing to leave Virginia and not return for at least twenty-five years. They

The Lovings answered questions at a press conference in June 1967, after the landmark Supreme Court ruling was handed down.

moved to nearby Washington, DC. They were both allowed to visit Virginia but never together. A condition of their suspended jail sentences forbade them from returning to the state as a couple.

The Civil Rights Movement

The Lovings married and were arrested in 1958. Their arrest happened about four years after the civil rights movement was thought to have started. The civil rights movement consisted of numerous protests, boycotts, and advocacy efforts, so it is difficult to say exactly when it began.

Before the civil rights movement, black people had few rights in the United States. After the Civil War, there was

Antimiscegenation at the State Level

In our system of government, federal laws are informed by the US Constitution. Often, though, important issues are handled at the state level. States are given free rein to determine their own laws on issues such as marriage.

Virginia was one of the first two states to establish laws criminalizing marriage between blacks and whites. These laws were called antimiscegenation laws. Along with Maryland, Virginia established antimiscegenation laws in the 1660s. At the time, Virginia and Maryland were still British colonies. Virginia's first laws dealt with marriage between whites and slaves or indentured servants. By 1691, Virginia had also passed legislation forbidding white people from marrying free black people. Similar laws were passed throughout the colonies, including in Pennsylvania, where many people opposed slavery. After the Revolutionary War, seven of the original thirteen colonies had laws banning interracial marriage. However, in 1780, Pennsylvania abolished its antimiscegenation law. In 1843, Massachusetts followed suit. This was a time of great growth in the United States. However, many of the new states passed antimiscegenation laws, even free states such as California. After the Civil War, several Southern states reversed their antimiscegenation laws. They were reinstituted shortly thereafter.

When the Lovings got married in 1958, twenty-four states had antimiscegenation laws. By the time the Supreme Court made the *Loving* decision in 1967, only sixteen states still had these laws on the books. Virginia was one of them. The court's ruling forced these states to overturn their laws and allow interracial marriage.

Interracial Marriage:
Loving v. Virginia

Linda Brown's father was responsible for the *Brown v. Board of Education* suit, which resulted in the desegregation of schools.

a period when the United States functioned under the "separate but equal" doctrine. A doctrine is a stated principle of legal or governmental policy. The "separate but equal" doctrine granted black citizens some of the same rights as white citizens. However, black citizens were kept separate from white citizens. The idea behind this legal doctrine was that people of color had to be granted access to the same types of facilities and services as white people. These facilities and services included housing, education, medical care, and transportation. White citizens, however, did not necessarily want black citizens to use the exact same facilities and services as them.

It was up to states and local governments to decide how they would enforce the doctrine. In Virginia, it was commonplace for accommodations and services to be segregated. Blacks and whites traveled on separate train cars and sections of the bus. They went to different schools. They used different public restrooms and drinking fountains. They ate in different restaurants and lived in different parts of town. There was very little intermingling between the races. In this era, interracial marriage was certainly frowned upon and often illegal.

The overall goal of the civil rights movement was to end racial segregation and discrimination against black citizens. The black community wanted to be offered the same constitutional rights and protections as white citizens. The services and facilities offered to black citizens were typically of a lower quality than the ones offered to white citizens. For example, schools for black children were often underfunded and staffed by teachers with no formal training or higher education. Schools for white children generally had adequate supplies and were staffed by teachers who had a formal education and training. The "separate but equal" doctrine was not working.

In a larger sense, "separate but equal" was an isolating doctrine. In the United States, it created a mindset that white citizens were still superior to black citizens. It also suggested that white citizens were entitled to far greater opportunities than black citizens. There was still the cultural idea that white and black citizens should not mix because white citizens were better than black citizens.

The landmark US Supreme Court case *Brown v. Board of Education of Topeka* began to change things. In 1954, the court ruled that segregated public schools were unconstitutional. This ruling marked the unofficial beginning of the civil rights movement. It began to break down racial barriers. It paved the way for a shift in laws governing interracial marriage.

Change in the United States was slow. *Brown v. Board of Education* certainly didn't mark the end of racism, which still exists in the United States today. It was, however, an important first step for racial equality.

Probably the most famous face of the civil rights movement was Martin Luther King Jr. As a leader, he supported nonviolent demonstrations and civil disobedience, a form of peaceful protest. In other words, King believed people should stand up against laws they thought were unjust or unfair. He helped organize sit-ins, boycotts, and marches. He also believed in the strength in numbers to help further the movement's message.

For example, King was involved in the March on Washington for Jobs and Freedom. The massive march in

Martin Luther King Jr. delivered his famous "I Have a Dream" speech at the March on Washington for Jobs and Freedom on August 28, 1963.

Washington, DC, took place on August 28, 1963. Roughly 250,000 people gathered to march for civil and economic rights for black citizens. More than 75 percent of the marchers were black. It was at this peaceful protest that King delivered his famous "I Have a Dream Speech" speech. The march is thought to have contributed to the passage of the Civil Rights Act of 1964. This act provided federal protections for minorities.

The era of the civil rights movement was not always peaceful, though. Famous human-rights activist Malcolm X did not agree with King's methods and peaceful protests. He also did not believe in racial integration, or the mixing of people of different races. Racial integration was something the civil rights movement hoped to bring about. Malcolm X and his followers believed that blacks and whites should remain separate. He believed in black supremacy. In other words, he felt black citizens were superior to white citizens.

Malcolm X had many followers. Those who followed him argued that his method of harshly confronting white people was more effective than the peaceful protests. Not surprisingly, white citizens did not agree with his belief in black supremacy. They were more motivated to buy into the idea of racial integration than they were to support the idea that black citizens were superior to white citizens.

Breaking Down Barriers

The movement toward racial integration was gaining steam with the civil rights movement. When the *Loving v. Virginia* case came before the Supreme Court, the civil rights movement undoubtedly factored into the Supreme Court's consideration of the case.

TWO

The Road to the Supreme Court

The United States court system has a series of steps that a case goes through before it reaches the US Supreme Court. The vast majority of legal cases never make it to the Supreme Court. They are adequately settled in a lower court. Sometimes, a case goes through all of the lower courts and no adequate resolution has been reached. When that happens, the case can be brought before the Supreme Court. The Supreme Court may or may not choose to hear the case. Typically, the cases they hear are ones where previous rulings may have violated the United States Constitution or ones where a ruling may have an effect nationwide.

This was the case with *Loving v. Virginia*. The Lovings' lawyers felt their arrests violated the Constitution. Their case touched on an issue that had been debated nationwide for more than a century. It was the exact type of case the Supreme Court typically hears.

The Arrest and Case

In 1924, Virginia passed the Racial Integrity Act. It required citizens in Virginia to register their race with the state. It was a felony to fake one's race on the registration. The crime

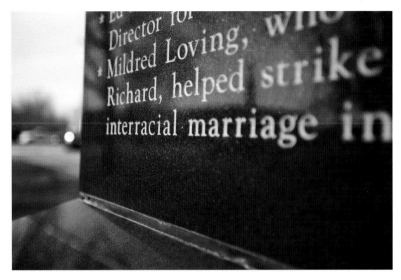

The Lovings are memorialized on a monument in Bowling Green, Virginia, for the role they played in striking down the Racial Integrity Act.

was punishable by one year in jail. The act also placed certain conditions on marriage related to race. The act stated that:

> It shall hereafter be unlawful for any white person in this State to marry any save a white person, or a person with no other admixture of blood than white and American Indian. For the purpose of this act, the term "white person" shall apply only to the person who has no trace whatsoever of any blood other than Caucasian; but persons who have one-sixteenth or less of the blood of the American Indian and have no other non-Caucasic blood shall be deemed to be white persons. All laws heretofore passed and now in effect regarding the intermarriage of white and colored persons shall apply to marriages prohibited by this act.

In other words, white people in Virginia could marry other white people who had no trace of blood from any other race. The exception was that they could marry another white person who had one-sixteenth or less Native American blood. Officials in marriage-license offices were allowed to refuse to grant a marriage certificate to a couple if they suspected either member of the couple was lying about his or her race. Mildred and Richard Loving traveled to Washington, DC, to get married because of this act.

Just five weeks after the Lovings married, they were asleep in their home when the police burst in. The police demanded to know whom Richard Loving had in the room with him. Mildred answered that she was his wife. Richard pointed to the couple's marriage certificate from Washington, DC. The sheriff announced that their certificate was not valid in Virginia.

Indeed, the sheriff was correct. Virginia law stated that interracial marriages performed outside of Virginia were invalid in Virginia. The Lovings were arrested. Richard spent the night in jail. Mildred spent several nights there.

The Lovings pled guilty to being in violation of the Racial Integrity Act. By doing so, they were able to accept a plea bargain. A plea bargain is a compromise between the prosecutor and the defendant in exchange for the defendant pleading guilty. In accordance with their plea bargain, the Lovings' one-year prison terms were suspended. The main condition of this bargain was that the Lovings had to leave Virginia. They also could not return together for at least twenty-five years. If they did return together, they would each go to prison.

Following through with the terms of the plea bargain, the Lovings moved to Washington, DC.

The First Appeal

Five years after their arrests, Mildred Loving decided to challenge the legal decision. She wanted to be able to visit family in Virginia with her husband. She also missed living in her home state.

She felt empowered by the civil rights movement. In particular, she felt motivated by the March on Washington, where Martin Luther King Jr. delivered his "I Have a Dream" speech. She wrote about her concerns to Attorney General Robert F. Kennedy. He suggested that she contact the American Civil Liberties Union (ACLU). The ACLU is an organization that focuses on protecting individuals' constitutional rights.

The ACLU believed the lower court's ruling was an attack on the Lovings' civil rights. The organization took the case and assigned lawyers Bernard S. Cohen and

The ACLU, which took on the Lovings' case, is still extremely active in fighting for people's civil rights.

Philip J. Hirschkop to represent the Lovings. The process was tricky, though. By pleading guilty in the original court case, the Lovings had lost their right to appeal, or petition for a reversal of a decision, at the lower-court level.

Cohen and Hirschkop filed a motion at the next level up: the Virginia Caroline County Circuit Court. Their motion asked the court to vacate, or cancel, the original judgments made when the Lovings were arrested. Cohen and Hirschkop requested this on the basis that the Racial Integrity Act was a violation of the Constitution. Specifically, it was a violation of the equal protection clause of the Fourteenth Amendment to the Constitution. Part of the amendment states:

> No State shall make or enforce any law which shall abridge the privileges or immunities of citizens of the United States; nor shall any State deprive any person of life, liberty, or property, without due process of law, nor deny to any person within its jurisdiction the equal protection of the laws.

In other words, no state can enforce a law that denies citizens of civil rights other citizens have. All citizens are also promised fair treatment by the courts. The Lovings were citizens of the United States. Their attorneys argued that denying mixed-raced couples the same rights to marry as white couples was a violation of the equal protections clause. In this way, the state of Virginia was denying citizens of color privileges that white citizens had.

The attorneys heard no response to their motion for almost a year. While they awaited a response, they filed a class-action suit, or a lawsuit filed on behalf of a larger group. They filed the class-action suit in hopes of getting Virginia's antimiscegenation laws declared unconstitutional. They filed the suit with the US District Court for the Eastern District of Virginia. District courts operate at the federal level, unlike lower courts. The lower courts typically operate at the state level. There is at least one district court in every state, though many states have multiple district courts. There currently are ninety-four district courts.

The class-action suit pushed the Virginia Caroline County Circuit Court to finally rule on the motion to vacate. The same judge who had ruled on the original case, Leon Bazile, ruled on the motion. In his opinion, or written legal decision, he wrote that God had intentionally placed people of different races on different continents so they would not marry. Judge Bazile believed that immigration was the only reason that people of different races were living on the same continent. He did not believe that was a part of God's plan.

Judge Bazile also cited *Kinney v. The Commonwealth* (1878) as legal precedent for his decision. The case was very similar to the *Loving* case. Andrew Kinney, a black man, and Mahala Miller, a white woman, went from Virginia to Washington, DC, to marry. In their case, the Virginia Supreme Court upheld the lower court's ruling. It ruled that the Kinneys would have to leave Virginia if they wanted to remain married.

Ultimately, Bazile stood his ground. He did not vacate the original conviction.

The Second Appeal

Cohen and Hirschkop were not discouraged by Judge Bazile's decision. After the attorneys received Bazile's decision, they appealed the case to the next court up. The next court was

The Supreme Court of Virginia is housed in the Old Finance Building in Richmond, Virginia.

the Virginia Supreme Court of Appeals, now known as the Supreme Court of Virginia. It is the highest court in Virginia. The US District Court for the Eastern District of Virginia, where the class-action suit was filed, postponed their decision while the Lovings took their case to the Supreme Court of Virginia. The attorneys argued that Judge Bazile's decision should be overturned based on the Lovings' constitutional rights.

In this case, known as *Loving v. Commonwealth*, the Supreme Court of Virginia upheld Bazile's ruling. The court agreed that the couple had violated Virginia's antimiscegenation laws. Justice Harry L. Carrico stated that the conviction was not a violation of the Lovings' rights under the equal protection clause. He believed it was not a violation

The Executive and Legislative Branches of Government

The US government has three branches: the judicial branch, the executive branch, and the legislative branch. The judicial branch includes the Supreme Court, as well as lower federal courts.

LEGISLATIVE

EXECUTIVE

JUDICIAL

These three branches make up the United States government.

The executive branch of government includes the president, vice president, and several cabinet departments. The executive branch makes sure the laws created by the legislative branch are carried out and enforced. Generally, the president can only sign a bill into law if it is first passed by the legislative branch. When the Lovings were arrested, Republican Dwight D. Eisenhower was president. When their case was brought before the Supreme Court, Democrat Lyndon B. Johnson was president. Johnson had signed the Civil Rights Act into law in 1964. He was open to ideas of desegregation, or the end of racial separation.

The legislative branch passes the laws that inform judgments made by the court system. The legislative branch includes both chambers of the United States Congress. The two chambers of Congress are the House of Representatives and the Senate. During the duration of the Lovings' court battles, the majority of members of Congress were Democrats.

because both of them were punished equally, regardless of their races. As precedent, he cited the 1883 Supreme Court ruling in *Pace v. Alabama*. That ruling upheld Alabama's antimiscegenation laws. The courts sentenced both a black man and a white woman to two years in prison for violating Alabama's law regarding interracial relationships.

The Supreme Court of Virginia did, however, alter the Lovings' sentence. Carrico believed that requiring the Lovings to leave Virginia was too stiff of a punishment. He felt that they should be able to return to the state. He also believed, however, they should no longer be allowed to live together as husband and wife.

The United States Supreme Court

The Lovings did not accept the Supreme Court of Virginia's ruling. They did not believe they were criminals. Despite Judge Bazile's original ruling, they wanted to be able to live in Virginia as husband and wife, so their attorneys took the case to the Supreme Court of the United States. It was there that history was made. After the Supreme Court heard the case, it delivered a landmark ruling that led to the end of antimiscegenation laws in the United States.

THREE

The Prosecution and the Defense

The Lovings had taken a small step forward in their legal case when their appeal was heard in the Supreme Court of Virginia. The court ruled that the punishment for the Lovings' crime had been too harsh. However, the Supreme Court of Virginia still felt that the Lovings were criminals who had violated the Racial Integrity Act.

The Lovings decided to take the final step and pursued their case in the United States Supreme Court. They were still represented by Bernard S. Cohen and Philip J. Hirschkop, on behalf of the ACLU,

The Lovings at home in Central Point, Virginia, with their children, Peggy, Donald, and Sidney

in the Supreme Court case. In fact, the Lovings did not even attend the court proceedings in Washington, DC. Instead, their lawyers argued the case on their behalf.

The Prosecution

Cohen and Hirschkop may have been relatively new to the legal profession, but they were both passionate about civil rights. The two of them put together a strong case on behalf of the Lovings.

Cohen summed up the case in its simplest terms. During his oral argument, he delivered a message from Richard Loving: "Tell the Court I love my wife and it is just not fair that I cannot live with her in Virginia." The Lovings were not necessarily interested in changing the face of marriage in the United States. They simply wanted to be allowed to live together as man and wife in their home state.

The Loving Dream Team

The Lovings were represented during appeal and at the Supreme Court level by two attorneys assigned by the ACLU: Philip J. Hirschkop and Bernard S. Cohen.

Hirschkop was born in Brooklyn but raised in New Jersey. While growing up in the New Jersey, he made friends with black migrant workers who sometimes shopped at his father's store. According to Hirschkop, some of his passion for social justice was due to his early interactions with these black workers.

Hirschkop attended Columbia University, where he studied mechanical engineering. He then obtained his law degree from Georgetown University. He was mentored by William Kuntsler, a well-known civil rights attorney. Kuntsler's influence contributed to Hirschkop's decision to become a civil rights lawyer. Hirschkop was also likely persuaded to become a civil rights attorney because

To Cohen, Hirschkop, and the ACLU, the case was about much more. While they were arguing on behalf of the Lovings, they were also arguing that the state's antimiscegenation laws were a violation of the Fourteenth Amendment. Hirschkop argued that the antimiscegenation laws were "slavery laws, pure and simple." He believed that the laws were in place in order "to hold the Negro class in a lower position, the lower social position, the lower economic position." In other words, the laws were in place to ensure

he witnessed the beatings of black citizens in the South. He had only been out of law school for a few years when he was assigned the *Loving* case.

Hirschkop's co-counsel was also born in Brooklyn. Bernard S. Cohen's experience as a Jewish man in New York inspired him to pursue a career as a civil rights attorney. Like Hirschkop, Cohen also received his law degree from Georgetown.

Cohen was one of the founders of the Virginia chapter of the ACLU. Like Hirschkop, he was only a few years out of law school when he was assigned

Philip Hirschkop, circa 1969

the *Loving* case. Cohen ended up presenting the oral argument on behalf of the Lovings in front of the Supreme Court.

that black Americans would be treated as second-class citizen. The treatment of black Americans as second-class citizens was a violation of the equal protection clause of the Fourteenth Amendment. The equal protection clause guarantees fair and equal treatment regardless of race.

The words and ideas of Martin Luther King Jr. were important to the lawyers arguing on behalf of the Lovings.

Hirschkop was echoing a sentiment Martin Luther King had expressed nearly a decade earlier. In 1958, King said, "When any society says that I cannot marry a certain person, that society has cut off a segment of my freedom." In other words, the right to marry was a basic liberty and right of every free citizen. To deny a person the right to marry was to deny him or her a part of his or her freedom.

Hirschkop pointed to actual slavery laws to support his argument that antimiscegenation laws were slave laws. For instance, he pointed to Virginia's 1691 Act for Suppressing Outlying Slaves. Hirschkop noted that the language of the 1691 act was important because it referred to interracial marriage. It stated that any who were found in an interracial marriage should be banished from Virginia. Indeed, the spirit of those early laws was similar to the Racial Integrity Act.

Since 1920, the ACLU has fought to protect people's constitutional rights. Hirschkop and Cohen argued that the Lovings' rights had been violated.

Hirschkop also referred to previous Virginia Supreme Court decisions. He mentioned *Kinney v. The Commonwealth* (1878) and *Naim v. Naim* (1955). In 1955, a white woman went before the Supreme Court of Virginia. She wanted to get an annulment, or legal invalidation, of her marriage to a Chinese man. She had married him three years prior. In accordance with Virginia's Racial Integrity Act, their interracial marriage was illegal. Her annulment was granted.

It might seem odd that Hirschkop referenced cases and acts where interracial marriage was banned or antimiscegenation laws were upheld. However, he was trying to make a point. Hirschkop argued that all of these earlier statutes and precedents robbed "the Negro race of their dignity." He went on to state that "fundamental in the concept of liberty in the Fourteenth Amendment is the dignity of the individual, because without that, there is no ordered liberty." In other words, robbing one group of their dignity destroys the foundation of liberty for all.

To support his argument for effectively "desegregating" marriage, Hirschkop cited *Brown v. Board of Education*. The 1954 Supreme Court case overturned laws that allowed states to have segregated schools for black and white students. The Supreme Court had unanimously decided that school segregation was unconstitutional. Hirschkop and Cohen hoped the court would make a similar decision about interracial marriage.

For his part, Cohen argued that the Lovings had been denied their constitutional right to due process, or fair treatment by the judicial branch. The Fourteenth Amendment contains a clause that states that no state can "deprive any person of life, liberty, or property, without due process of law." Cohen argued that the right for citizens to

Linda Brown and her sister Terry Lynn at their segregated school circa 1953, before the *Brown v. Board of Education* decision

marry is a liberty protected by the due process clause. He believed that the Lovings had not been treated fairly by the courts because of their different races. He also argued that antimiscegenation laws were "arbitrary and capricious," or random and inconsistent.

Since the equal protection and the due process clauses are both part of the Fourteenth Amendment, Hirschkop's and Cohen's arguments were very closely tied together. Hirschkop laid the groundwork by speaking first in front of the court. Then Cohen addressed specifically how the *Loving* case and antimiscegenation laws were a violation of the due process clause. Both Hirschkop's and Cohen's arguments boiled down to one simple fact. Black people were being treated differently than white people under the law. They argued that this was a violation of the Constitution, which guarantees all citizens equal rights.

The Defense

The state of Virginia was represented by Robert McIlwaine. He was an attorney for the state attorney general's office. McIlwaine served as defense counsel for the state of Virginia in other civil rights cases as well. In the 1950s and 1960s, he appeared before the Supreme Court for cases regarding school desegregation and redistricting. McIlwaine was known for arguing that Virginia's laws should be upheld on the basis of states' rights.

McIlwaine had legal precedent on his side in *Loving v. Virginia*. There were numerous earlier cases upholding interracial marriage bans and antimiscegenation laws. For instance, in 1922, the Arizona Supreme Court granted a white man an annulment from his wife (*Kirby v. Kirby*). He had requested the annulment because he learned she was "of negro blood." Similarly, in 1939, the California Court of Appeals invalidated the marriage between Allan Monks and Antoinette Giraudo after Monks's death. The court invalidated the marriage because Monks was white and Giraudo was one-eight black. This resulted in Giraudo not being entitled to Monks's estate, or money and property, after his death.

Despite strong legal precedent, McIlwaine focused on the fact that the Fourteenth Amendment does not specifically forbid states from having antimiscegenation laws. He argued that the men who drafted the Fourteenth Amendment had considered interracial marriage. He argued that the writers had intentionally not stated anything about antimiscegenation laws.

Robert McIlwaine represented Virginia at the Supreme Court hearing.

Chief Justice, or head judge, Earl Warren asked McIlwaine how he had come to this conclusion. McIlwaine replied that it was implied by the debates that led up to the drafting of the Fourteenth Amendment. Those debates also involved the passage of the Civil Rights Act of 1866. The act was similar to the Fourteenth Amendment. McIlwaine stated that:

> By the time the ... Civil Rights Act of 1866 had been debated and passed, the issue of whether or not the ... Civil Rights Act of 1866 would infringe the power of the states to pass antimiscegenation statutes was so completely settled, that when the Fourteenth Amendment resolution was brought on, the question was no longer considered to be an open one.

In other words, it was a nonissue. The drafters of the
Fourteenth Amendment had agreed that states could
individually make decisions about antimiscegenation
laws. McIlwaine did not think there was a reason to
change that view.

McIlwaine's view was that of an originalist, or a person
who argues that the Constitution and its amendments should
be understood as the people who wrote them intended.
In this view, the Constitution cannot be interpreted based
on changes in history and society over time. The opposite
view is that the Constitution and its amendments are living
documents. In that way, their meanings and how they are
applied can change as society changes.

Constitutional originalist McIlwaine was arguing against
ACLU attorneys Hirschkop and Cohen. McIlwaine had
precedent on his side. The two ACLU attorneys had the
civil rights movement on theirs. Would the justices of the
Supreme Court adopt the originalist view? Or would they
take into account the civil rights movement? Would they
adopt the idea that the Constitution and its amendments are
living documents?

FOUR

The Court's Ruling

Ultimately, the Supreme Court ruled in favor of the Lovings. But why? What made the justices rule in favor of the Lovings, even with so much precedent supporting states' rights to ban interracial marriage? Even though the civil rights movement was well under way and desegregation had begun, the United States was still a very segregated country. In many parts of the country, it was still frowned upon for blacks and whites to mix.

The Makeup of the Court

To understand the court's decision, it's helpful to look at the justices at that time. The Supreme Court is made up of one chief justice and eight associate justices. The chief justice is the judge who serves as the spokesperson for the judicial branch.

The chief justice during the *Loving v. Virginia* case was Earl Warren. He was a California native who attended the University of California, Berkeley. The university was known for its civil rights activity in the 1950s and 1960s. Although Warren attended Berkeley long before that time, UC Berkeley has long been known as a forward-thinking university. Warren was a Republican. However, he was known

The United States Supreme Court building in Washington, DC

for his liberal decisions on the court. For instance, he was the chief justice for the *Brown v. Board of Education* decision.

The associate justices on the court were Hugo Black, William J. Brennan Jr., Thomas C. Clark, William O. Douglas, Abraham Fortas, John M. Harlan II, Potter Stewart, and Byron White.

Hugo Black was a Democrat from Alabama. He served as a United States senator before serving on the Supreme Court. Alabama supported antimiscegenation laws. In fact, Alabama was the last state to officially remove its antimiscegenation statutes, in 2000. However, Black was a strong supporter of civil rights and liberal policies. At the time of the *Loving* case, he was the most experienced Supreme Court justice. He had served on the court since 1937.

William Joseph Brennan Jr. was a Democrat born in New Jersey. He was definitely on the liberal side of the court. In fact, he was known as being a highly outspoken progressive.

The justices who heard the *Loving* case: *(clockwise from top left)* White, Brennan, Stewart, Fortas, Harlan, Douglas, Warren, Black, and Clark

Thomas Campbell Clark was a Texas-born Democrat. Texas favored antimiscegenation laws. However, Clark voted in favor of civil liberties in a number of cases involving racial segregation, including *Brown v. Board of Education*. In 1964, he wrote the majority opinion, or written decision agreed on by the majority of the justices, for *Heart of Atlanta Motel v. United States*. This case established that private businesses must abide by the Civil Rights Act of 1964.

Like Black, William Orville Douglas had served the court a long time. He was appointed to the Supreme Court in 1939. Douglas was a Democrat from Minnesota. Minnesota was one of the few states to never pass antimiscegenation laws. Douglas tended to favor liberal decisions as well. In 1975, *Time* magazine said he was "the most ... committed civil libertarian ever to sit on the court." In other words, he was one the biggest supporters of liberal policies in the court's history.

John Marshall Harlan II was a Chicago-born Republican. His grandfather had also served on the Supreme Court. He was a Rhodes Scholar who studied at Oxford University in England. Harlan was a conservative member of the court. He typically did not vote to overturn legislation. However, he also felt that the Fourteenth Amendment protected civil rights not specifically stated in the Constitution.

Potter Stewart was also a Republican. He was from Michigan. He tended toward the center of the court. This meant that he did not necessarily always vote conservative or liberal. However, he usually voted in favor of civil rights in the cases that came before the court.

Byron Raymond White was a Democrat born in Colorado. Before joining the court, he played professional football and

Chief Justice Earl Warren

Earl Warren was the chief justice of the Supreme Court when the *Loving* case was heard. Warren was born in California on March 19, 1891. He was the child of Scandinavian immigrants. His father was a railroad worker. He was murdered during a robbery when Warren was a teenager. Warren went on to earn a bachelor's degree in political science from UC Berkeley in 1912. He then received a law degree from the same university in 1914.

Warren entered politics after World War I. He became governor of California in 1943 and served three terms. Warren had aspirations of becoming president of the United States. That dream ended during the 1952 presidential election when loyalties among politicians changed. Instead, President Dwight D. Eisenhower appointed Warren to the Supreme Court in 1953. The Senate unanimously confirmed, or approved, him in 1954.

Eisenhower was a Republican like Warren. Republicans tended to be on the more conservative side of politics. However, Warren was known for his

Chief Justice Earl Warren, circa 1966

liberal decisions on the Supreme Court. He supported the end of segregation in schools (*Brown v. Board of Education*). He was in favor of ending school-sponsored prayer in public schools (*Engel v. Vitale*). He also helped protect the rights of people accused of crimes (*Gideon v. Wainwright* and *Miranda v. Arizona*).

worked for John F. Kennedy's 1960 presidential campaign. It was hard to classify White as either conservative or liberal. He tended to form opinions on a case-by-case basis. He did not necessarily commit to one ideology, or a system of ideas that forms an economic or political theory and policy. However, he did tend to vote in favor of civil rights. He fully supported desegregation of schools. He also supported affirmative action policies, which strive to offer more opportunities for minorities and victims of discrimination.

Abraham Fortas was a Tennessee-born Democrat. He had a great interest in children's legal rights and juvenile justice. He relied on the Fourteenth Amendment to give rights to children and juveniles that previously had not been granted.

Given the makeup of the Supreme Court in 1967, the decision in *Loving v. Virginia* is not entirely surprising. Under Chief Justice Earl Warren, the court was largely liberal. Even those justices who were on the conservative side tended to rule in favor of civil rights. Many of the justices were also born and raised in states that had abolished (or never had) antimiscegenation laws. Only a couple of justices sitting on the bench were from the Deep South. In the South, antimiscegenation laws and sentiments still ran deep. As the justices considered the case before them, the civil rights movement certainly did not go unnoticed.

If the court had been largely conservative, the outcome of the case might have been different. The civil rights movement and the arguments of Hirschkop and Cohen might still have won the case for the Lovings. However, it is also possible that a more conservative court might have been persuaded by legal precedent and McIlwaine's argument. They might have upheld Virginia's right to enforce the Racial Integrity Act.

During the civil rights movement, picketing was a common form of peaceful protest. Here, the NAACP pickets over school segregation.

The Court Speaks

Defense attorney Robert McIlwaine focused much of his argument on his belief that the Fourteenth Amendment should be interpreted as the writers of the amendment likely intended it. He also claimed that it was reasonable for states to ban interracial marriage. He argued that states have a "natural, direct, and vital interest in maximizing the number of successful marriages which lead to stable homes and families and in minimizing those which do not." In other words, he claimed that states benefited from successful marriages. McIlwaine stated that mixed-race couples faced "greater pressures and problems" than same-race marriages. Since they faced more pressures, they were more likely to result in unstable homes.

The justices on the court were skeptical of this claim. They questioned McIlwaine about what sources he used to develop it. They also pointed out the slippery slope of McIlwaine's argument. It was impossible to tell if unstable mixed-race marriages led to a perceived need for antimiscegenation laws. It may have been that antimiscegenation laws led society to believe that interracial marriages were undesirable. Chief Justice Warren commented that people might have similar views about marriages between people of different religions. Warren worried that if states were allowed to prohibit one type of marriage, then they would be allowed to prohibit others. Where was the line drawn in terms of these laws being a violation of the Fourteenth Amendment?

Justice Black pointed out that antimiscegenation laws left a black man "bound to feel that he is not given equal protection of the laws." It would also make a black man feel "that the white man was superior to the colored man." He stated that the "Fourteenth Amendment was adopted to prevent" that exact sentiment.

Chief Justice Warren also pointed out the hypocrisy in the Racial Integrity Act. The act prevented black people and people of any race other than white from marrying white people. It did not prevent people of races other than white from intermarrying. Warren asked, "If [the Racial Integrity Act] is to preserve the purity of the races, why aren't [races

Justice Hugo Black, circa 1955

other than white] as much entitled to have purity of their races protected as a white race?" In other words, if the law was really about keeping the races from mixing, then the law should prevent all people, not just white people, from marrying people from other races.

Ultimately, the court's ruling was unanimous. There were no dissenting, or opposing, opinions from the justices. On June 12, 1967, the court delivered their landmark decision.

The words of the Fourteenth Amendment are memorialized at the
Brown v. Board of Education National Historic Site in Topeka, Kansas.

All of the justices agreed that Virginia's Racial Integrity Act
violated the due process and equal protection clauses of the
Fourteenth Amendment of the Constitution.
    In the written opinion, Chief Justice Warren noted:

> The Equal Protection Clause requires the
> consideration of whether the classifications drawn
> by any statute constitute an arbitrary and invidious
> discrimination. The clear and central purpose of the
> Fourteenth Amendment was to eliminate all official

state sources of invidious racial discrimination in the States. There can be no question but that Virginia's miscegenation statutes rest solely upon distinctions drawn according to race ... There can be no doubt that restricting the freedom to marry solely because of racial classifications violates the central meaning of the Equal Protection Clause.

In other words, Warren was stating that the equal protection clause protects people from random and unjust discrimination. He believed Virginia's law preventing people from marrying based on race was a violation of this clause.

The court's decision also touched on the violation of the due process clause. The justices all agreed that marriage was "one of the 'basic civil rights of man.'" They also agreed that "to deny this fundamental freedom ... is surely to deprive all the State's citizens of liberty without due process of law." In other words, to deny someone the right to marry was to deny

The Justices and Their Votes

Question: Did Virginia's antimiscegenation law violate the equal protection clause of the Fourteenth Amendment?

Yes: Black, Brennan, Clark, Douglas, Fortas, Harlan, Stewart, Warren, White

No: (none)

that person of fair and equal treatment by the judicial system. The justices went on to agree that "under our Constitution, the freedom to marry, or not marry, a person of another race resides with the individual, and cannot be infringed by the State." The court believed that it was every individual's right to decide whether or not to marry someone of a different race. The justices also believed that this right could not be taken away by a state's laws.

That last line prohibiting state interference went beyond just Virginia's Racial Integrity Act. It made antimiscegenation laws in every other state that still had them unenforceable. With the Supreme Court's decision that states' antimiscegenation laws were unconstitutional, there was no longer any gray area. Throughout the United States, interracial marriage could not be prohibited.

The fact that the decision was unanimous spoke volumes about the progress that had been made due to the civil rights movement. The court sent a clear message that depriving a person of basic human rights based on race was unconstitutional.

FIVE

The Legacy of *Loving* v. Virginia

Whenever the Supreme Court delivers a landmark decision, the effects are felt far and wide. They influence future legal decisions at the local, state, and federal levels. They also contribute to societal change. The *Loving v. Virginia* ruling has had those types of effects.

Societal Change

Before the *Loving* case, interracial marriage was negatively viewed in many states. At the time of the case, views were changing in some states. These views were changing mainly in the western and northern United States. States in the Deep South still tended to hold strong antimiscegenation views. For example, Alabama continued to have antimiscegenation laws as part of its state constitution until November 2000. It even tried to enforce its laws until 1970. Although the state could not enforce its antimiscegenation statues, they remained on the state's constitution. An amendment to remove the invalid ban was only met with about 60 percent approval from Alabama voters. This meant that, in 2000, about 40 percent of Alabamans believed there should still be a ban on interracial marriage.

Interracial Marriage:
Loving v. Virginia

Loving v. Virginia paved the way for future civil rights cases, such as cases fighting for same-sex marriages.

Interracial marriage is commonly accepted now, though there are parts of the country where it is not as common as it is in larger metropolitan areas.

Even though societal change has been slow, it has been steady. According to a Pew Research Center study, only 3 percent of newlyweds nationwide were in an interracial marriage in 1967. In 2015, nearly fifty years after the *Loving* decision, that number had increased more than five times, to 17 percent.

However, the rate of interracial marriage does vary depending on location. Interracial marriage is more common in large metropolitan areas. It is also not nearly as common in some of the Southern cities. For instance, in Jackson,

45

Interracial Marriage:
Loving v. Virginia

White supremacist rallies still take place, but there are often counter-protests by people invested in protecting civil rights and liberties.

Mississippi, the percentage of interracial marriages was just 3 percent in 2015. That was the same percentage in 2015 in Jackson as the national percentage in 1967. In parts of the country considered more liberal and with a more varied mix of races and backgrounds, the rate is much higher. For instance, Los Angeles, California, is more ethnically diverse than Jackson, Mississippi. The rate of interracial marriages in Los Angeles was 22 percent in 2015.

The legalization of interracial marriage nationwide has also helped to slowly erode white supremacist views in the United States. White supremacy is the belief that white people are superior to people of other races. In the *Loving* ruling, the justices mentioned several times that antimiscegenation laws were put in place to ensure white supremacy. They noted how this was a violation of the Fourteenth Amendment.

The *Loving* ruling did not instantly erase white supremacy in the United States. White supremacist sentiments still exist in this country. However, the ruling communicated that black citizens and other people of color were to be treated the same as white people. The civil rights movement was a great contributor to this change, of course. The *Loving* victory was a piece of that larger movement. It helped to support equality among all races in the United States.

Legal Influence

In a legal sense, the *Loving* ruling stretched beyond making states' antimiscegenation laws unenforceable. The *Loving* ruling paved the way for other Supreme Court decisions. Namely, it aided in the Supreme Court's 2015 ruling that overturned states' bans on same-sex marriages (*Obergefell v. Hodges*).

The issue of same-sex marriage had been debated for some time. Same-sex marriage was a controversial issue for many of the same reasons interracial marriage had been in the 1950s and 1960s. In fact, the *Loving v. Virginia* case was cited in a California case that overturned the state's ban on same-sex marriage in 2010 (*Perry v. Schwarzenegger*). In a societal sense, same-sex couples wanted the stigma removed from being in same-sex relationships. They also wanted to enjoy the same legal rights as married heterosexual couples made up of a husband and a wife. For instance, marriage offers tax benefits, property rights, government benefits, and immigration benefits. Married couples also receive parenting rights. That means that both people in the couple have legal

Overturning a State Law

*L*oving v. Virginia was not only used as legal precedent for same-sex marriage cases. In 1970, it informed the decision in *United States v. Brittain*. In that case, Sergeant Louis Voyer and Phyllis Bett wanted to get married in Alabama. Voyer was a white man and Bett was a black woman. Although the *Loving* ruling had come down three years before, Voyer and Bett were denied a marriage license by Judge G. Clyde Brittain. He stated that Alabama law said such a license would be criminal. Indeed, Brittain was correct. At that time, the Alabama state constitution forbade lawmakers from legalizing marriage between a white person and a black person.

However, federal law replaces state law when a federal ruling exists. Once the case reached the federal district court, Judge Brittain's ruling was quickly overturned. The US Constitution is the supreme law of the land in the United States. Since the Supreme Court had already ruled that banning interracial was unconstitutional, it was no surprise that Voyer and Bett won the right to marry.

Same-sex couples celebrated the Supreme Court's ruling on marriage equality by legally marrying.

rights over their children. Similarly, married couples have rights of survivorship, which means rights if one partner dies. These are just a few examples of benefits heterosexual couples enjoyed but same-sex couples did not while states refused to legally recognize same-sex marriages. When states began to overturn their bans on same-sex marriage, it was a major turning point for lesbian, gay, bisexual, transgender, and queer (LGBTQ) rights.

In California, the case that overturned the ban was *Perry v. Schwarzenegger.* Judge Vaughn Walker of the United States District Court for the Northern District of California cited the *Loving* case as precedent. He stated that "an individual's exercise of his or her right to marry no longer depends on his or her race nor on the race of his or her chosen partner." He concluded that "the freedom to marry is recognized as a fundamental right protected by the Due Process Clause." Walker was pointing to the fact that the *Loving* decision protected marriage as a fundamental right. Since it was protected that anyone can marry anyone else regardless of race, then a person should also be able to marry anyone of any sex.

In 2014, other courts followed suit. Marriage bans were struck down in Alaska, Arizona, Colorado, Idaho, Indiana, Kansas, Montana, Nevada, North Carolina, Oklahoma, Oregon, South Carolina, Utah, Virginia, West Virginia, Wisconsin, and Wyoming.

The *Loving* case was also used as precedent when considering whether to overturn the same-sex marriage bans in Kentucky, Michigan, Ohio, and Tennessee. These states ultimately ruled against overturning the bans. They believed the Supreme Court's decision in *Loving v. Virginia* only applied to marriage between heterosexual partners.

Even as states' same-sex marriage bans were being upheld, same-sex couples could travel to another state to marry. These couples faced the same problem that Mildred and Richard Loving faced. Their marriage licenses obtained in a different state would not be legally recognized in their home states. When *Obergefell v. Hodges* went to the Supreme Court in 2015, thirteen states still had same-sex marriage bans in effect. These states were Arkansas, Georgia, Kentucky, Louisiana, Michigan, Mississippi, Missouri, Nebraska, North Dakota, Ohio, South Dakota, Tennessee, and Texas.

The Supreme Court ruling in *Obergefell v. Hodges* came about in part because of different decisions in several federal courts. *Obergefell v. Hodges* was a case specifically from Ohio. However, it was combined with three other cases challenging state same-sex marriage bans and related issues when it went before the Supreme Court in 2015. These other cases were *DeBoer v. Snyder*, which challenged Michigan's ban on adoption by same-sex couples; *Bourke v. Beshear*, which challenged Kentucky's same-sex marriage ban; and *Tanco v. Haslam*, which challenged Tennessee's same-sex marriage ban. Collectively, the cases came before the Supreme Court as *Obergefell v. Hodges*.

The Supreme Court ruled that states must legally allow same-sex couples to marry. In the Supreme Court's written opinion, Justice Anthony Kennedy cited the *Loving* case numerous times. The court stated:

> A first premise of the Court's relevant precedents is that the right to personal choice regarding marriage is inherent in the concept of individual autonomy. This abiding connection between marriage and liberty is why ... in *Loving* the Court invalidated a prohibition on interracial marriage under both the Equal Protection Clause and the Due Process Clause.

In other words, the antimiscegenation laws were overturned because the Supreme Court saw them as a violation of the equal protection and due process clauses

When Barack Obama was president, the White House lit up in rainbow colors to celebrate the Supreme Court decision in *Obergefell v. Hodges*.

of the Fourteenth Amendment. Same-sex marriage bans were overturned because the Supreme Court saw them as a violation of the same parts of the Fourteenth Amendment.

The Future

Some people argue that allowing same-sex marriage is a slippery slope that could result in more types of marriage being allowed. For instance, those people are concerned about polygamy, or the practice of having more than one spouse at the same time. Similarly, those people are concerned about marriages in which at least one member of the couple is not yet a legal adult. Around the time of the *Loving* decision, similar "slippery slope" arguments were made against allowing interracial marriage. However, many people view the Supreme Court decisions on interracial and same-sex marriage simply as steps forward in the fight for equality. These decisions ensured that the civil rights of all United States citizens are respected. It would not be surprising if the *Loving* ruling was used as precedent in future civil rights cases.

Chronology

1878 The Vriginia Supreme Court upholds the state's rules preventing interracial marriages (*Kinney v. The Commonwealth*).

1883 The US Supreme Court upholds states' rights to enforce antimiscegenation laws (*Pace v. Alabama*).

1896 The US Supreme Court rules that the segregation of public facilities is constitutional, establishing the "separate but equal" precedent (*Plessy v. Ferguson*).

1922 The Arizona Supreme Court upholds antimiscegenation statutes by granting an annulment to a white man who had married a woman of black ancestry (*Kirby v. Kirby*).

1924 The Racial Integrity Act of 1924, designed to further prevent interracial marriages, is passed in Virginia.

1948 The California Supreme Court overturns a state ban on interracial marriage because it was a violation of the Fourteenth Amendment of the Constitution (*Perez v. Sharp*).

1954 The US Supreme Court deems separate public schools for black and white students unconstitutional (*Brown v. Board of Education of Topeka*).

1955 The Virginia Supreme Court grants a white woman an annulment from a Chinese man in accordance with the Racial Integrity Act (*Naim v. Naim*).

1964 The US Supreme Court unanimously rules that it is unconstitutional to prohibit the cohabitation of two people of opposite sexes if one is black and the other white (*McLaughlin v. Florida*).

1967 The US Supreme Court unanimously rules states' antimiscegenation laws are unconstitutional (*Loving v. Virginia*).

1970 A district court rules that Alabama's state antimiscegenation laws are unenforceable because of the *Loving v. Virginia* decision (*United States v. Brittain*).

2010 A district court overturns California's ban on same-sex marriage (*Perry v. Schwarzenegger*).

2015 The US Supreme Court rules that bans on same-sex marriage are unconstitutional (*Obergefell v. Hodges*).

Glossary

affirmative action Policies in areas such as hiring and college admissions that level the playing field for people who are members of a group that has historically been discriminated against.

annulment The legal invalidation of a marriage.

antimiscegenation laws Laws that criminalize marriage between people who are from different racial backgrounds.

appeal To apply to a higher court for the reversal of a decision made in a lower court.

black supremacy The belief that black people are superior to people of other races.

civil disobedience A form of peaceful protest in which people refuse to comply with certain laws.

class-action suit A lawsuit filed by a person or a small group of people on behalf of a larger group.

desegregation The end of racial segregation, or the separation of people because of race.

doctrine A stated principle of legal or governmental policy.

due process Fair treatment by the judicial system.

ideology A system of ideas that forms the basis of economic or political theory and policy.

interracial Between or involving more than one race.

LGBTQ An acronym used to collectively describe the community that includes people who identify as lesbian, gay, bisexual, transgender, or queer.

opinion A formal statement, given by a court, on the reasons for the court's judgment.

polygamy The custom or practice of having more than one spouse at the same time.

precedent A previous legal case or decision that is used to decide similar cases in the future.

racial integration The mixing of people or groups who were previously separated due to their different races.

redistricting Dividing an area into new political districts. This practice can be used to influence the outcome of elections.

vacate To cancel or annul a previous judgment.

white supremacy The belief that white people are superior to people of other races.

Further Information

Books

Cates, David. *Plessy v. Ferguson: Segregation and the Separate but Equal Policy.* North Mankato, MN: Essential Library, 2012.

Fremon, David K. *The Jim Crow Laws and Racism in United States History.* New York: Enslow Publishing, 2014.

Porterfield, Jason. *Marriage Equality: Obergefell v. Hodges.* New York: Enslow Publishing, 2017.

Torres, John A., and Harvey Fireside. *Desegregating Schools: Brown v. Board of Education.* New York: Enslow Publishing, 2017.

Van Zee, Amy. *Dred Scott v. Sandford: Slavery and Freedom Before the American Civil War.* North Mankato, MN: Essential Library, 2012.

Websites

PBS Black Culture Connection
http://www.pbs.org/black-culture/home

This PBS website allows visitors to explore black history and culture through stories, films, and television shows.

Supreme Court of the United States

https://www.supremecourt.gov

The Supreme Court website has an extensive collection of oral arguments, opinions, history, and more.

United States Courts

http://www.uscourts.gov

This website contains information about the US court system and has a useful educational resources section.

Videos

Loving vs. Virginia

https://www.youtube.com/watch?v=0Vbwylnshuo

The Lovings' story and the Supreme Court case was fictionalized in the novel *Loving v. Virginia: A Documentary Novel of the Landmark Civil Rights Case*. This video contains a discussion of the book and the landmark case.

Obergefell v. Hodges Supreme Court Oral Arguments

https://www.youtube.com/watch?v=Hdj4d6_u4M8

This video contains audio from the oral arguments for *Obergefell v. Hodges*.

Supreme Court Clips: *Loving v. Virginia*

https://www.youtube.com/watch?v=zfAxFgr8I28

This video presents clips from the arguments in *Loving v. Virginia*.

Selected Bibliography

"An Act for Suppressing Outlying Slaves." Library of Virginia: Encyclopedia Virginia, September 30, 2011. https://www.encyclopediavirginia.org/_An_act_for_ suppressing_outlying_slaves_1691.

Bazile, Leon M. "Opinion of Judge Leon M. Bazile (January 22, 1965)." Library of Virginia: Encyclopedia Virginia, March 25, 2014. https://www.encyclopediavirginia.org/ Opinion_of_Judge_Leon_M_Bazile_January_22_1965.

"Intermarriage Across the U.S. by Metro Area." Pew Research Center, May 18, 2017. http://www.pewsocialtrends.org/ interactives/intermarriage-across-the-u-s-by-metro-area.

King, Martin Luther, Jr. *The Papers of Martin Luther King, Jr., Volume IV: Symbol of the Movement, January 1957– December 1958.* Berkeley: University of California Press, 2000.

"Kirby v. Kirby." Arizona Supreme Court, May 2, 1922. https://www.ravellaw.com/ opinions/81b00409e9ab9272979200b0f5caad60.

"The Law: The Court's Uncompromising Libertarian." *Time,* November 24, 1975. http://content.time.com/time/ magazine/article/0,9171,913732-2,00.html.

Martin, Douglas. "Mildred Loving, Who Battled Ban on Mixed-Race Marriage, Dies at 68." *New York Times*, May 6, 2008. http://www.nytimes.com/2008/05/06/us/06loving.html.

"Perry v. Schwarzenegger." United States District Court for the Northern District of California. Accessed December 30, 2017. https://ecf.cand.uscourts.gov/cand/09cv2292/files/09cv2292-ORDER.pdf.

"Racial Integrity Act Documents." Library of Virginia: Racial Integrity Laws. Accessed December 30, 2017. https://lva.omeka.net/items/show/128.

Rothman, Lily. "A History Lesson for the Kentucky Clerk Refusing to Grant Marriage Licenses." *Time*, September 1, 2015. http://time.com/4018494/kentucky-marriage-clerk-loving-virginia.

United States District Court, N. D. Alabama, E. D. "*United States v. Brittain* Ruling." District Court, ND Alabama, December 8, 1970. https://scholar.google.com/scholar_case?case=4101369272554922509&.

US Supreme Court. "Decision on *Loving v. Virginia* (June 12, 1967)." Library of Virginia: Encyclopedia Virginia, April 9, 2014. https://www.encyclopediavirginia.org/Loving_v_Virginia_June_12_1967.

US Supreme Court. "Opinion of the Court: *Obergefell v. Hodges*." June 26, 2015. https://www.supremecourt.gov/opinions/14pdf/14-556_3204.pdf.

Index

Page numbers in **boldface** are illustrations.

About the Author

Cathleen Small is an editor and the author of dozens of nonfiction books for students grades three through twelve. She is also a legislative advocate active in the pursuit of equality and civil rights for citizens with disabilities. When she's not writing or advocating, Small enjoys traveling and spending time with her husband and their two sons.